Esercizi di comprensione del testo in inglese

Italian - Polish

____

Let's Read & Color Together

My Favorite Teacher

disegno

Drawing

colorazione

Coloring

contento

Happy

insegnante

Teacher

My Favorite Teacher

disegno

rysunek

colorazione

kolorowanie

contento

szczęśliwy

insegnante

nauczyciel

Reading Comprehension

My Favorite Teacher

Mis Avera is my favorite teacher. I like her because she is kind and helpful. She helps me with my drawing and coloring. She cheers me up and makes me happy if I miss mommy and daddy in school. Miss Avera is also charming. She is a tall lady. She has long, dark brown hair. She is the best teacher in the world.

The text is about

A. teachers in school

B. drawing and coloring in the school

C. Miss Avera, the writer's beloved teacher

A detail that tells about the main idea is

A. Miss Avera is short.

B. Miss Avera makes the writer happy.

C. Miss Avera helps the writer to read and write.

The Little Toy Boat

vela  Sail	oceano  Ocean
barca  Boat	rocce  Rocks

The Little Toy Boat

vela

żagiel

oceano

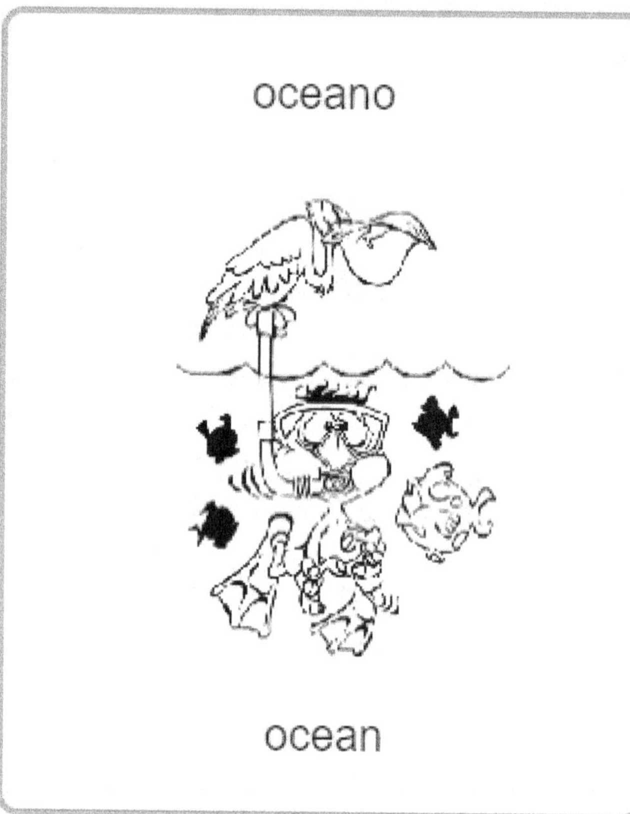

ocean

barca

łódź

rocce

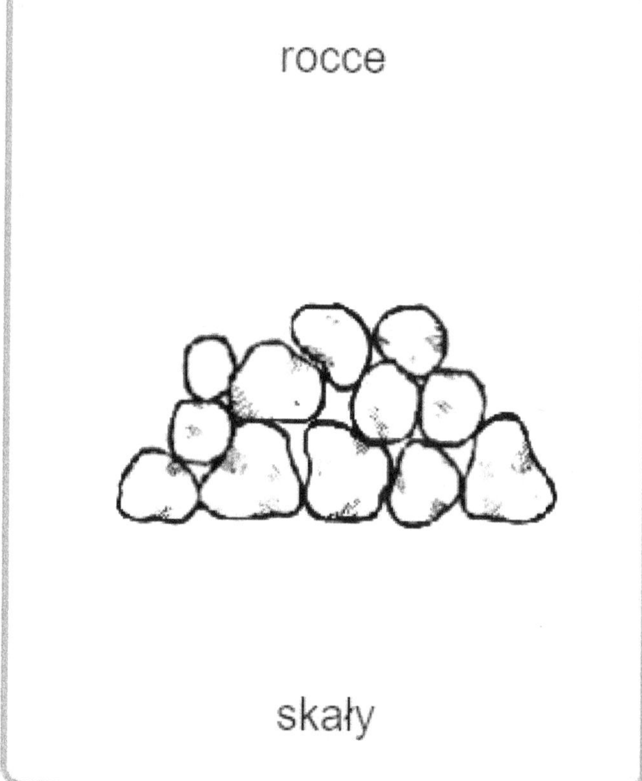

skały

The Little Toy Boat

Minnie loves to take baths. That is when she can play with her little toy boat. She puts it in the water. Then she splashes in the water to make small waves in the bath. The little boat looks like it sailing in a big ocean. It rocks from side to side, but it never sinks. Minnie loves her tiny boat.

The text is about

A. the waves in the bath

B. Minnie's little toy boat

C. a boat sailing in the ocean

A detail that tells about the main idea is

A. Minnie's boat sails in the ocean.

B. Minnie's toy boat rocks from side to side.

C. Minnie enjoys bathing.

Happy Mommy with Premium Coffee

caffè

Coffee

tazza

Cup

mattina

Morning

bere

Drink

Happy Mommy with Premium Coffee

caffè

Kawa

tazza

Puchar

mattina

ranek

bere

drink

Reading Comprehension

Happy Mommy with Premium Coffee

Gemmy's mother enjoys drinking premium coffee. She drinks coffee every day. When she wakes up in the morning, she drinks one cup of coffee. In the afternoon, she drinks two cups of coffee. In the evening, she drinks another cup. She has to buy coffee once a week from the supermarket.

The text is about

A. drinking tea every day

B. Gemmy's mother is enjoying drinking coffee.

C. buying coffee every week

A detail that tells about the main idea is

A. Gemmy's mother drinks coffee once a week.

B. Gemmy has a cup of coffee in the morning.

C. Gemmy's mother has one cup of coffee in the morning.

How to Bowl Better

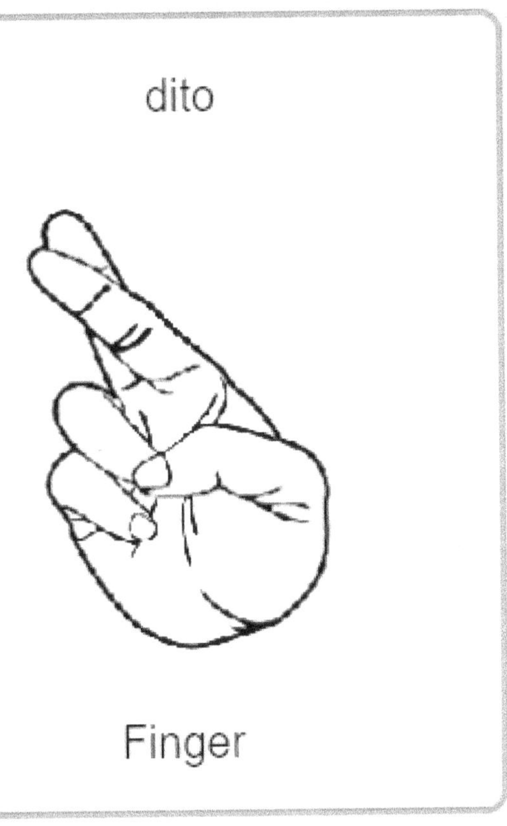

dito

Finger

mano

Hand

gettare

Throw

bowling

Bowling

How to Bowl Better

dito

palec

mano

dłoń

gettare

rzucać

bowling

kręgle

How to Bowl Better

Today is Chad's first day of learning how to bowl. First, he takes the bowling ball in two hands. Next, he places her fingers into the ball. Then he swings and throws the ball. Chad knocks down four pins on his first try. Good job, Chad!

The text is about

A. learning to play a new game

B. Chad's first try at bowling

C. bowling as a sport

A detail that tells about the main idea is

A. Chad knocks down four pins of his first throw.

B. Bowling is hard.

C. Chad uses his feet to bowl.

School Sparkling Shoes

sporco

Dirty

buco

Hole

acquistare

Buy

negozi

Shops

School Sparkling Shoes

sporco

brudny

buco

otwór

acquistare

kupować

negozi

sklepy

Reading Comprehension

School Sparkling Shoes

Faith needs a new pair of shoes for school. Her old pair torn. Her old shoes have many holes in them. They are also very dirty. Today Faith goes to the shoe shop with her mother. Her mother buys her a new pair of shoes. They are shimmering white. Faith is looking forward to school on Monday.

The text is about

A. Faith needing a new pair of shoes

B. Faith going to school on Monday

C. Faith going to the shops with her mother

A detail that tells about the main idea is

A. Faith's old shoes torn.

B. Faith's old shoes are clean.

C. Faith does not like school.

Circus Is Fun For Everyone

scimmia

Monkey

leone

Lion

elefante

Elephant

palla

Ball

Circus Is Fun For Everyone

scimmia

małpa

leone

Lew

elefante

słoń

palla

piłka

Circus Is Fun For Everyone

The Mario circus is in town. There are monkeys, lions, and elephants at the circus. The animals in the Mario circus are unique. They can do many tricks. The elephants can play with colorful balls. The monkeys can ride small bicycles. All the children can't wait to visit the Mario circus.

The text is about

A. animals in a circus

B. the Mario special circus

C. the circus being in town

A detail that tells about the main idea is

A. There are monkeys, snakes, and giraffes at the circus.

B. The elephants can play with sticks.

C. The monkeys can ride bicycles.

Fun Playground Near Me

cursore

Slider

altalene

Swings

casa

House

giardino

Garden

Fun Playground Near Me

cursore

suwak

altalene

huśtawki

casa

dom

giardino

ogród

Reading Comprehension

Fun Playground Near Me

There is a beautiful playground next to my house. It has a slide, a see-saw, and a swing. I enjoy playing on the see-saw. It is yellow. I like the see-saw because it goes up and down. I am pleased when I am playing on the see-saw.

The text is about

A. the writer enjoying the playground

B. the writer's see-saw in his garden

C. the writer's first visit to the playground

A detail that tells about the main idea is

A. The writer enjoys playing on the see-saw.

B. The playground has a slide, see-saw, and merry-go-round.

C. The playground is far away from the writer's house.

My First-Time Picnic

picnic

Picnic

cestino

Basket

sandwich

Sandwich

formaggio

Cheese

My First-Time Picnic

picnic

piknik

cestino

kosz

sandwich

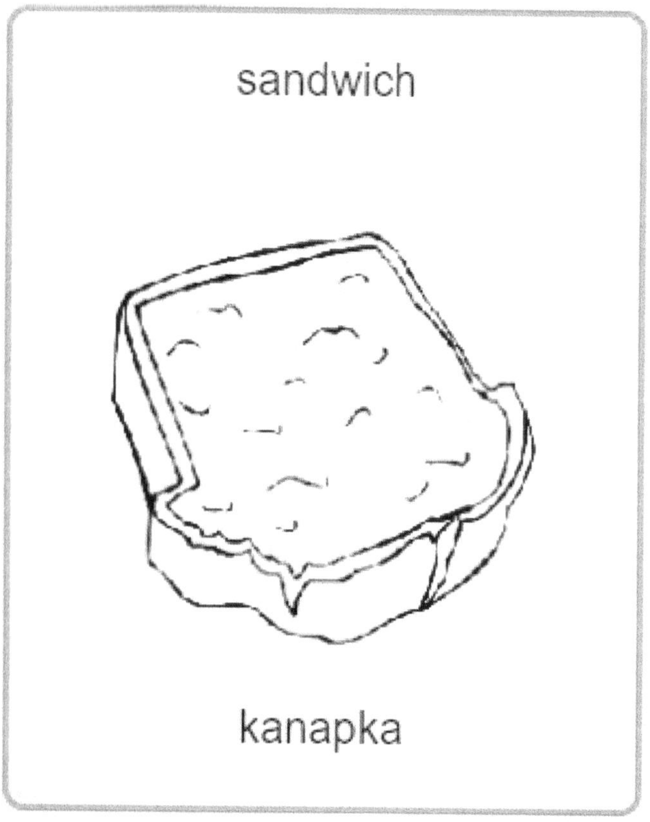

kanapka

formaggio

ser

My First-Time Picnic

It is a beautiful morning. Lydia is going for a picnic. She is taking a picnic basket with her. She has a red picnic basket. It is a big basket. In the basket, Lydia has some cold orange juice, salad, cheese sandwiches, and a slice of blueberry pie. Lydia is excited about her first-time picnic.

The text is about

A. Lydia going on a picnic

B. Lydia and her food

C. fun at picnics

A detail that tells about the main idea is

A. Lydia's food is in a big box.

B. Lydia has drinks and food in her picnic basket.

C. Lydia thinks she will not enjoy her picnic.

I Want to Be a Nurse!

infermiera

Nurse

malato

Sick

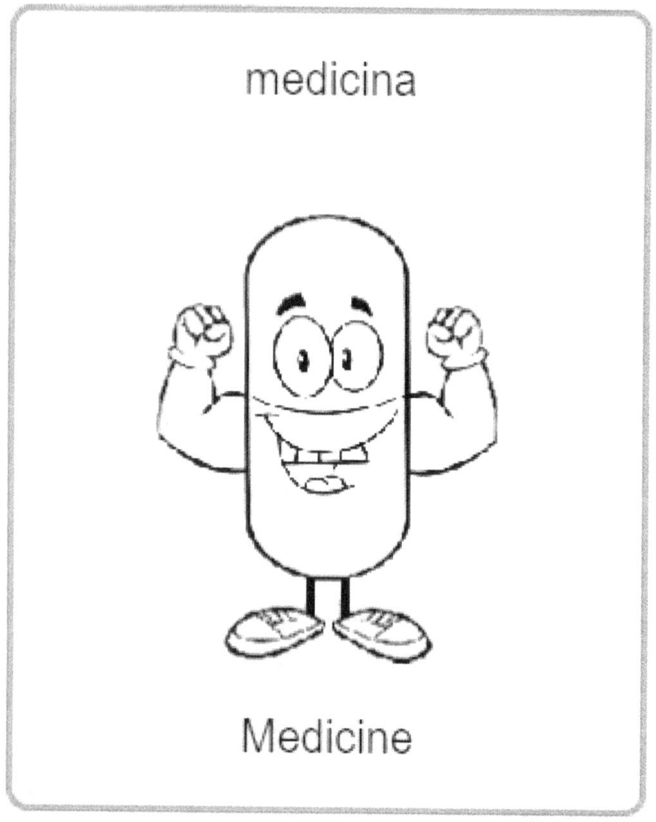

medicina

Medicine

imparare

Learn

I Want to Be a Nurse!

infermiera

pielęgniarka

malato

chory

medicina

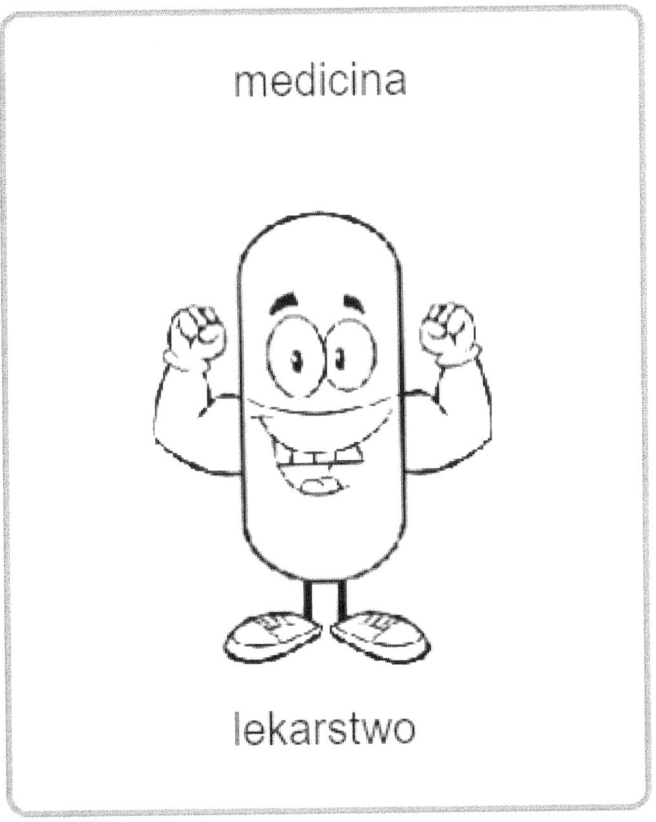

lekarstwo

imparare

uczyć się

I Want to Be a Nurse!

Jane has always wanted to be a nurse. She has to do a three-year course to train as a nurse. She will have to learn how to take care of sick people. She will also have to learn to give them medicine. Jane is looking forward to becoming a nurse.

The text is about

A. becoming a nurse

B. Jane's nurse

C. giving medicine

A detail that tells about the main idea is

A. Jane has to take a three-year course.

B. Jane needs to learn how to make medicine.

C. Jane does not like nursing.

My Gentle Daddy

papà

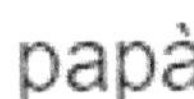

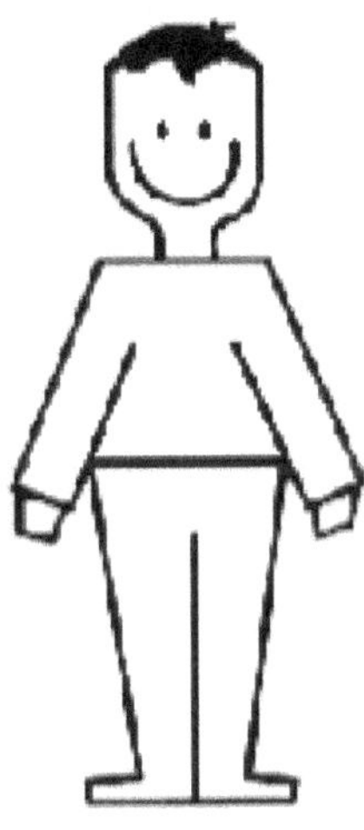

Daddy

casa

Home

calcio

Football

ciclismo

Cycling

My Gentle Daddy

papà

tatuś

casa

Dom

calcio

piłka nożna

ciclismo

Jazda rowerem

My Gentle Daddy

My daddy loves me very much. He plays games and football with me when he comes home from work. Sometimes we play hind and seek in the field. On other days, we go cycling. When daddy is tired, we go for a walk in the park. I love my daddy. He is the best daddy in the world.

The text is about

A. good fathers

B. the writer's love for his daddy.

C. walking, cycling and playing football

A detail that tells about the main idea is

A. His daddy is very busy at work.

B. They don't spend time together.

C. He goes for walks, cycles and plays football with his daddy.

Wind, Wind, Blow Away

freddo

Cold

amico

Friend

sciarpa

Scarf

albero

Tree

Wind, Wind, Blow Away

freddo

zimno

amico

przyjacielu

sciarpa

szalik

albero

drzewo

Wind, Wind, Blow Away

It was a cold and windy day. Pete was going to meet his friend. He put on his leather hat. Then he tied a woolly scarf around his neck. He was all set. Then, a strong gust of wind blew his hat off. Up and up it went. It eventually landed on top of a tree!

The text is about

A. Pete's scarf

B. Pete's hat getting blown away

C. Pete's meeting with his friend

A detail that tells about the main idea is

A. He tied a scarf around his neck.

B. The hat landed on top of a tree.

C. Pete was all set to meet his friend.

My Best Friend Forever

capelli

Hair

scuola

School

cibo

Food

giocattoli

Toys

My Best Friend Forever

capelli

włosy

scuola

szkoła

cibo

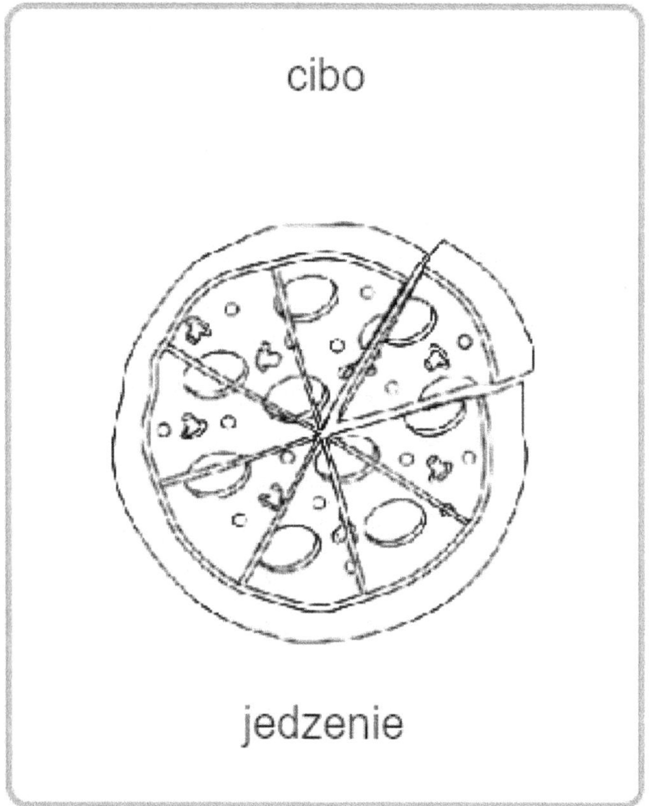

jedzenie

giocattoli

zabawki

Reading Comprehension

My Best Friend Forever

My best friend's name is Lisa Park. She is tall and thin. She has long black hair. She likes to tie her hair into two pigtails. She is a lovely person. In school, she always shares her snack and toys with me. Lisa and I do everything together. Every day we eat, play, and read books together. I hope we will always be friends.

The text is about

A. sharing toys

B. good friends

C. Lisa, the writer's best friend.

A detail that tells about the main idea is

A. They always fight.

B. Lisa ties her hair in a ponytail.

C. They eat, play, and read books together every day.

pittura

Painting

nave

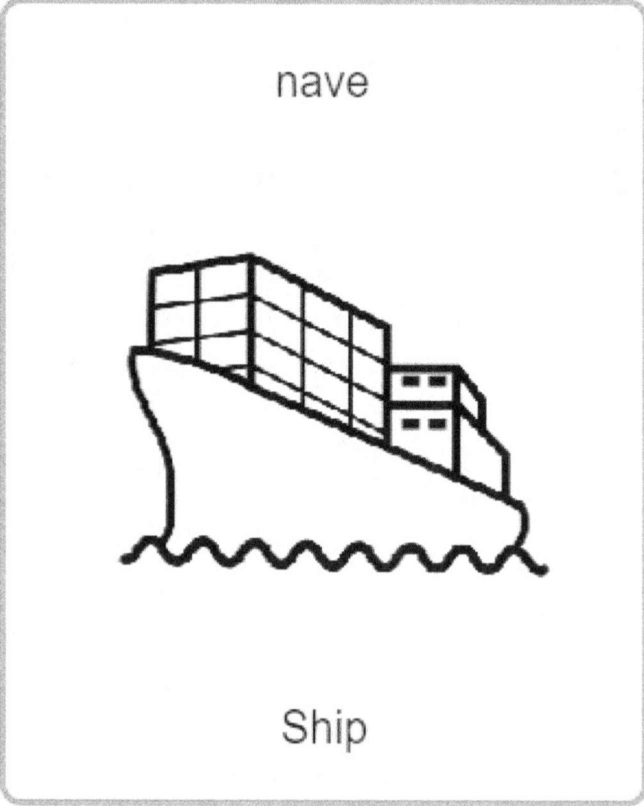

Ship

immagine

Picture

pittore

Painter

Painting like Pro!

pittura

obraz

nave

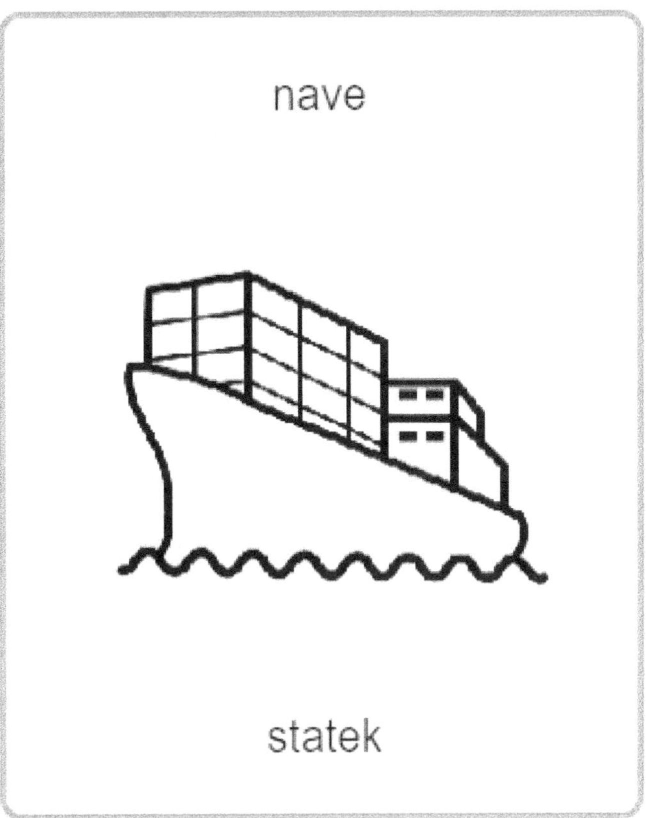

statek

immagine

obrazek

pittore

malarz

Painting like Pro!

Daniel wants to be a famous painter like Vincent van Gogh. He loves painting colors on canvas. Wherever he goes, he collects different paint colors. He now has blue, yellow, green, black, and orange paints. The latest picture he painted was a ship. His teacher said it was excellent.

The text is about

A. painting ships

B. Daniel's love for painting

C. Vincent van Gogh

A detail that tells about the main idea is

A. Daniel likes painting on paper.

B. Daniel only loves to paint ships.

C. Daniel paints in many different paint colors.

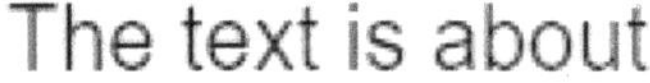

Rainbow Around the Sun

arcobaleno

Rainbow

pioggia

Rain

sole

Sun

bellissimo

Beautiful

Rainbow Around the Sun

arcobaleno

tęcza

pioggia

deszcz

sole

słońce

bellissimo

piękny

Rainbow Around the Sun

Joon saw a rainbow today. The rainbow appeared after the rain. Joon tried to count the different colors in that rainbow. Some of these colors were blue, red, yellow, green, and orange. Red is the most vivid color in the rainbow. Red is also Joon's favorite color in the rainbow.

The text is about

A. the colors of a rainbow

B. Joon's favorite color

C. the beautiful rainbow Joon saw

A detail that tells about the main idea is

A. Joon saw blue, red, yellow, green, and orange in the rainbow.

B. Joon's favorite color in the rainbow is blue.

C. Joon does not like rainbows.

Bun Bun the Lovely Cat

occhi

Eyes

gatto

Cat

letto

Bed

parete

Wall

Bun Bun the Lovely Cat

occhi

oczy

gatto

kot

letto

łóżko

parete

ściana

Bun Bun the Lovely Cat

My cat's name is Bun Bun. It is a yellow and orange cat. He sleeps on my bed every night. He is also smart. He can do tricks with a tiny ball and climb very high walls. I love Bun Bun very much.

The text is about

A. Bun Bun the dog

B. Bun Bun the cat

C. neighborhood cats

A detail that tells about the main idea is

A. Bun Bun has black eyes.

B. Bun Bun is a yellow and orange cat.

C. Bun Bun is lazy.

My Warm Family

famiglia

Family

sorella

Sister

gattino

Kitten

cane

Dog

My Warm Family

famiglia

rodzina

sorella

siostra

gattino

kotek

cane

pies

Reading Comprehension

My Warm Family

A family can be of any size. My family is big. I have a brother named Joe. My sisters' names are Jane, Jan, and June. We live in a big house with my parents and grandparents. We also have pets in our family. We have a big dog name Jab. Our little kitten's name Jam.

The text is about

A. the writer's big family

B. a small family

C. pets in the writer's family

A detail that tells about the main idea is

A. The writer has three sisters.

B. The writer has two brothers.

C. The writer does not live with her grandparents.

Fun Races for Sports Day

ragazzo

Boy

medaglia

Medal

saltare

Jump

genitori

Parents

Fun Races for Sports Day

ragazzo

chłopak

medaglia

medal

saltare

skok

genitori

rodzice

Fun Races for Sports Day

Eli is a very active and energetic little boy. Today was a sports day at his school. He enjoyed sports day very much. Eli won three medals at his sports day. He won a gold medal for the Sack Race. He won a silver medal for the 30-meter sprint. He also won a bronze medal for a group Tug of War. Eli's parents were very proud of him.

The text is about

A. sports at school

B. Eli's experience at sports day

C. Eli's parents

A detail that tells about the main idea is

A. Eli won two medals on sports day.

B. Eli participated in a group tug of war.

C. Eli's parents were unhappy with him.

Big School Bus Experience

autobus

Bus

fermare

Stop

autista

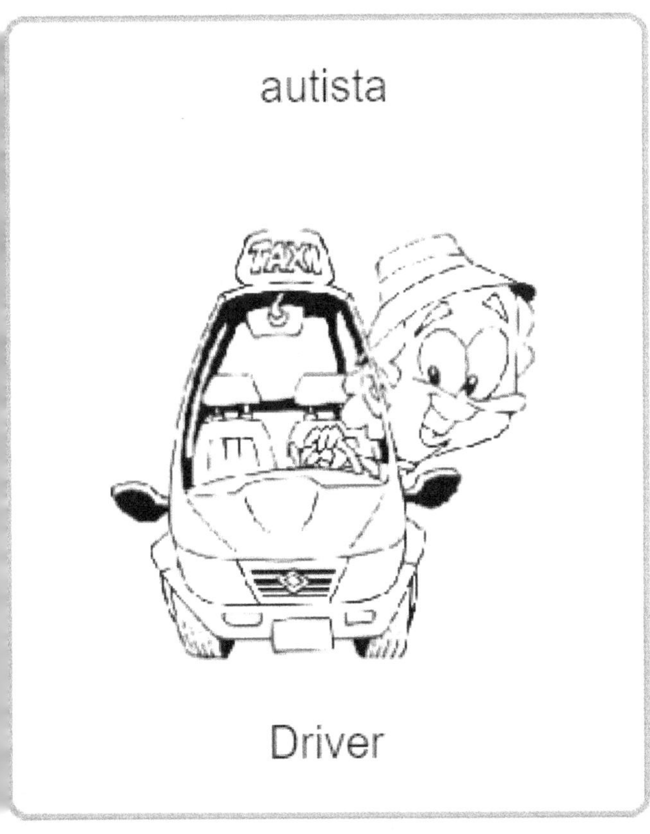

Driver

nervoso

Nervous

Big School Bus Experience

autobus

autobus

fermare

zatrzymać

autista

kierowca

nervoso

nerwowy

Reading Comprehension

Big School Bus Experience

Today was Paul's first day of taking the school bus. He was very excited. He was afraid he would lose his way. He waited at the bus stop. When he saw the bus, he put his hand out to stop it. When the bus stopped, Paul slowly climbed onto the bus. He said, "Good morning" to the bus driver. When he took his seat, he sighed with relief.

The text is about

A. Paul's first day at school

B. Paul's first time taking the school bus

C. taking the school bus

A detail that tells about the main idea is

A. Paul was happy.

B. Paul was afraid of losing his way.

C. Paul asked the bus driver for help.

Great Time with Sing Along

cantare

Sing

cantante

Singer

insegnante

Teacher

lei

She

Great Time with Sing Along

cantare

śpiewać

cantante

piosenkarz

insegnante

nauczyciel

lei

Ona

Reading Comprehension

Great Time with Sing Along

Elsa has a beautiful voice. She can sing very well. Elsa sings everywhere she goes. She sings in her school choir. Her choir teacher thinks Elsa has a lovely voice. She says Elsa sounds like a bird. She makes Elsa the lead singer.

The text is about

A. Elsa's choir teacher

B. joining the choir

C. Elsa's beautiful voice

A detail that tells about the main idea is

A. Elsa sings at home.

B. Her teacher says Elsa sings like a bird.

C. Elsa is not in the choir.

Oh Pretty Baby My Little Baby

bambino

Baby

affamato

Hungry

bottiglia

Bottle

triste

Sad

Oh Pretty Baby My Little Baby

bambino

niemowlę

affamato

głodny

bottiglia

butelka

triste

smutny

Oh Pretty Baby My Little Baby

Baby John is my younger brother. He is three months old. He is normally a happy baby. But when he is hungry, he begins to cry. It makes me sad to see him cry. When my mother gives him his milk, he stops crying. I love my brother very much.

The text is about

A. crying babies

B. baby John

C. milk bottles

A detail that tells about the main idea is

A. Baby John is always crying.

B. Baby John is a happy baby.

C. Baby John is six months old.

Affy's Birthday Cake

torta

Cake

fragola

Strawberry

candela

Candle

compleanno

Birthday

Affy's Birthday Cake

torta

ciasto

fragola

truskawka

candela

świeca

compleanno

urodziny

Affy's Birthday Cake

My sister, Affy, is three years old today. My parents gave her a birthday cake. It is a strawberry and chocolate cake. The cake is pink and brown. It has little flowers on it. There are a small yellow candle on the cake.

The text is about

A. birthday cakes

B. Affy's birthday cake

C. Affy, my friend's sister

A detail that tells about the main idea is

A. The cake is yellow.

B. The cake has small flowers on it.

C. There are three candles on the cake.

Enjoy Big Breakfast

marmellata

Jam

uovo

Egg

latte

Milk

prima colazione

Breakfast

Enjoy Big Breakfast

marmellata

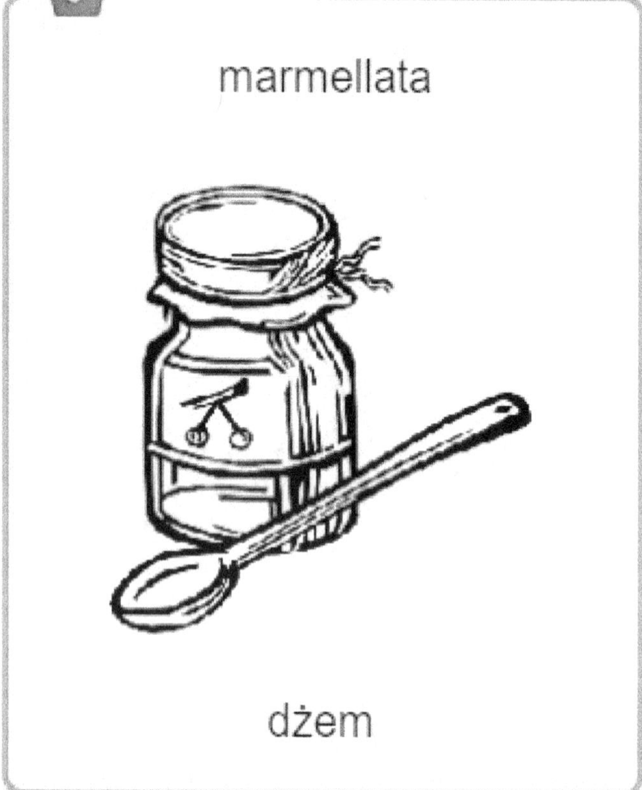

dżem

uovo

jajko

latte

mleko

prima colazione

śniadanie

Enjoy Big Breakfast

Andy enjoys having a big breakfast. He has two slices of toast with butter and strawberry jam. He also has a plate of scrambled eggs. Some mornings, he has bacon and pumpkin soup too. He finishes his breakfast with a big glass of hot chocolate. He is full once he finishes eating.

The text is about

A. eating a good breakfast

B. Andy has a large breakfast.

C. having eggs for breakfast

A detail that tells about the main idea is

A. Andy does not eat breakfast.

B. Andy eats two slices of bread with butter and jam.

C. Andy is still hungry after eating breakfast.

It's a Wonderful Bath Time

bagno

Bath

piangere

Cry

bolla

Bubble

acqua

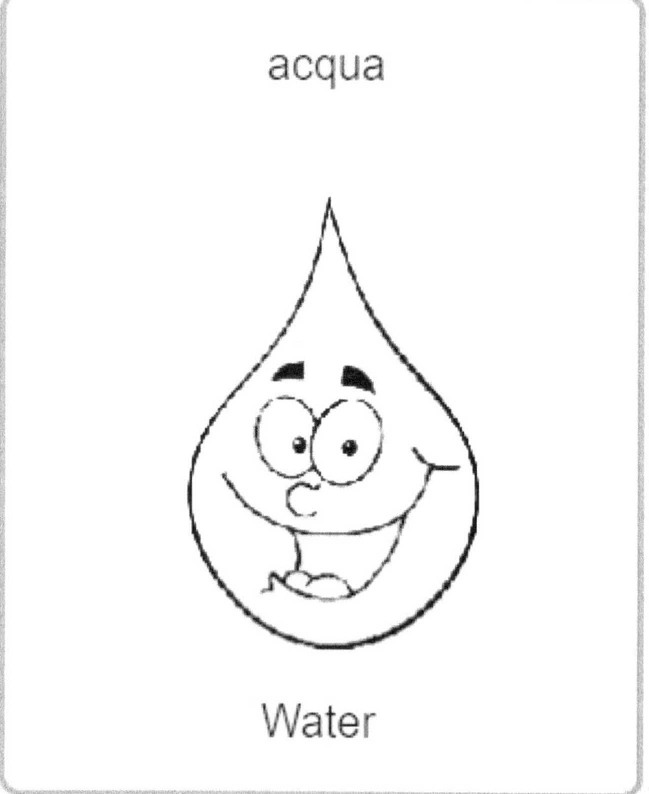

Water

It's a Wonderful Bath Time

bagno

kąpiel

piangere

płakać

bolla

bańka

acqua

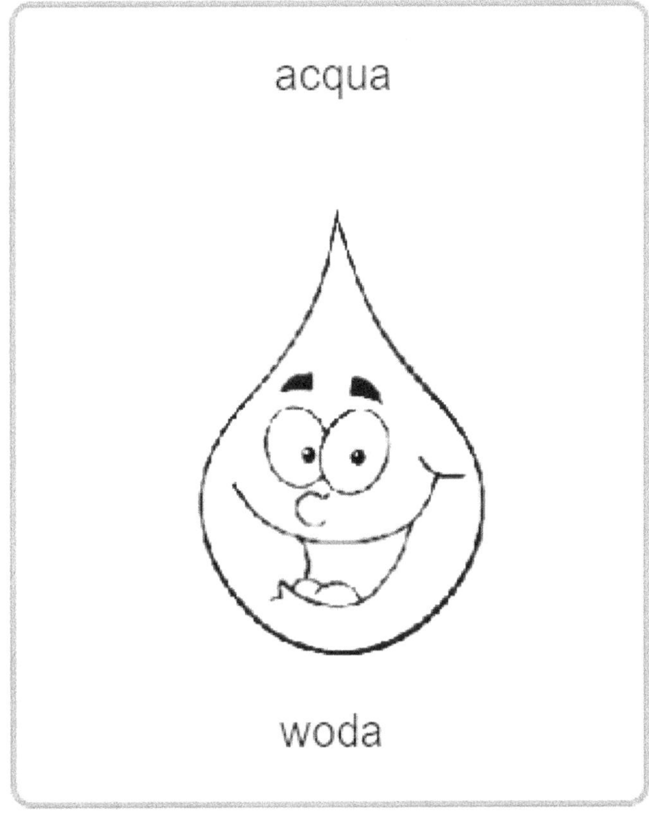

woda

Reading Comprehension

It's a Wonderful Bath Time

Tee always enjoys his bath time. He does not cry when he has his bath. He loves to play with the bubbles in the bathtub. There are also four rubber crabs in Tee's bath. He usually fills them up with water and lets them float around him. It makes Tee squeal with a laugh.

The text is about

A. rubber ducks in the bath tub

B. Tee having fun during bath time

C. bathing

A detail that tells about the main idea is

A. Tee cries while bathing.

B. There are plastic ducks in his bathtub.

C. Tee squeals with a laugh while bathing.

A Fun Christmas Party

natale

Christmas

camicia

Shirt

sorriso

Smile

regali

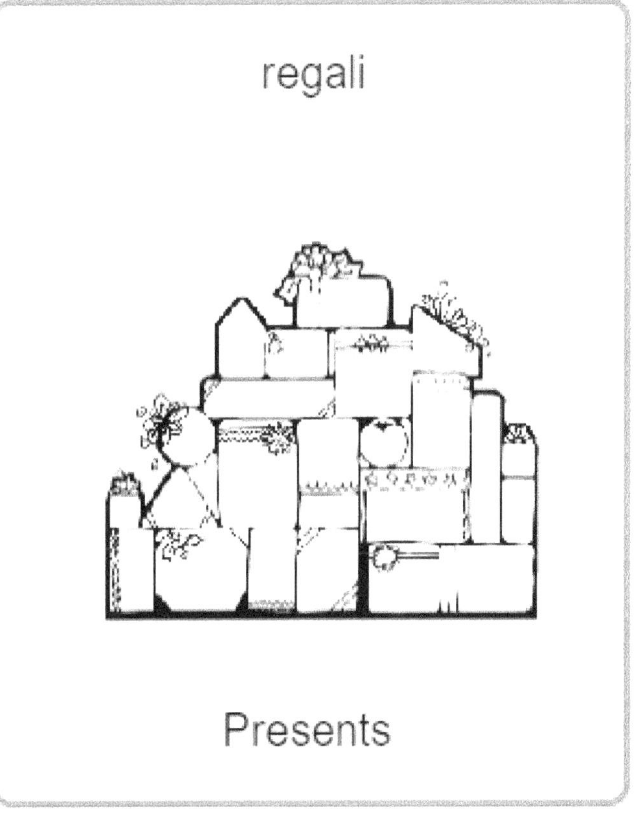

Presents

A Fun Christmas Party

natale

Boże Narodzenie

camicia

koszula

sorriso

uśmiech

regali

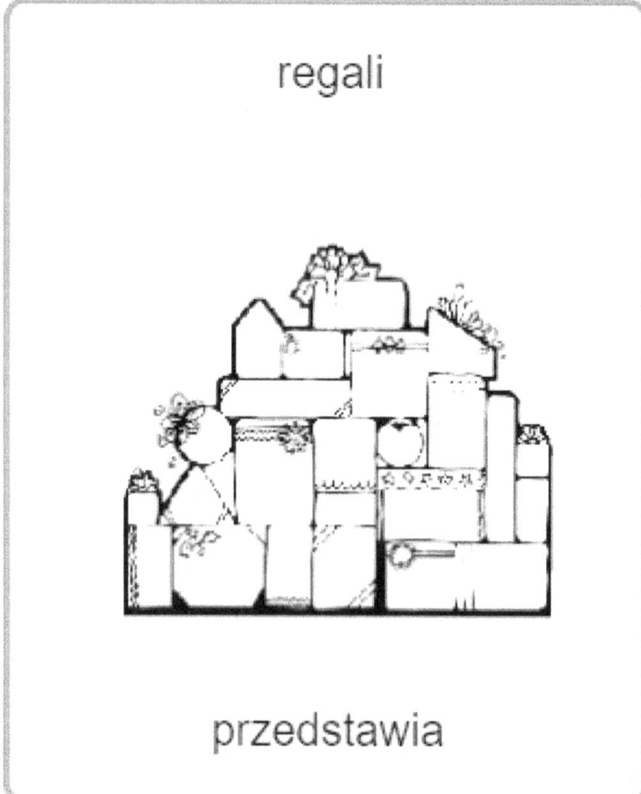

przedstawia

A Fun Christmas Party

Gemmy and Affy are going to a Christmas party. They are wearing blue and pink shirts. They are taking some presents for the party. They will give them to their friends. They are also taking some cheesecakes and fruit pies for the party. They are very excited. They have big smiles on their faces.

The text is about

A. blue and pink Christmas clothes

B. Christmas parties around the world.

C. The Christmas party Gemmy and Affy are going to.

A detail that tells about the main idea is

A. Gemmy and Affy are sad.

B. Gemmy and Affy are taking some salad to the party.

C. Gemmy and Affy are wearing blue and pink clothes.

Tom's Kite

aquilone

Kite

nastro

Ribbon

uccello

Bird

cielo

Sky

Tom's Kite

aquilone

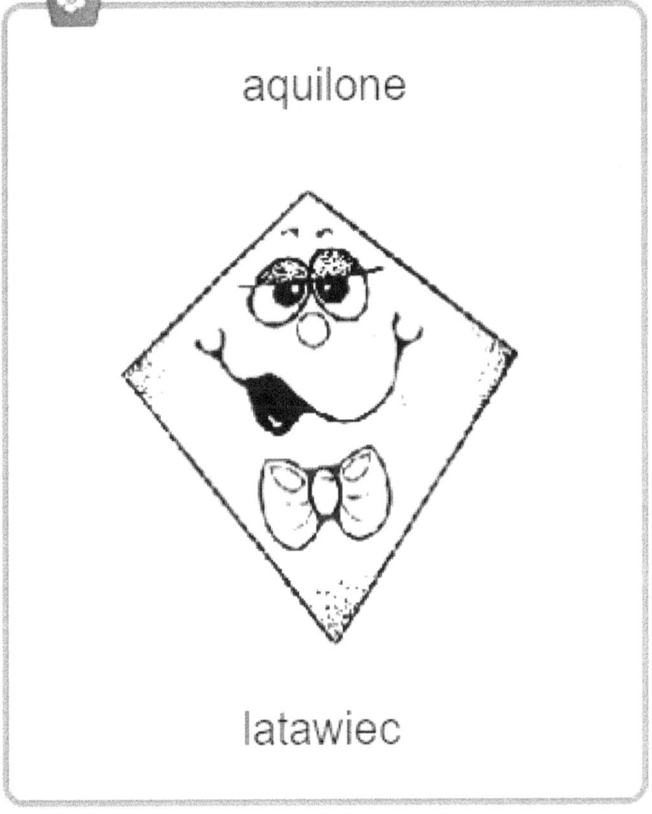

latawiec

nastro

faborek

uccello

ptak

cielo

niebo

Tom's Kite

Tom loves to fly kites. When he has time, he goes to the open field near his house. He flies his diamond-shaped kite. It is very big, and it has ribbons on the end. Tom thinks it looks like a huge bird in the sky.

The text is about

A. The open field near Tom's house

B. The ribbons on Tom's kite

C. Tom's kite

A detail that tells about the main idea is

A. Tom likes to go to the field.

B. Tom likes to look at birds.

C. Tom thinks his kite looks like a bird in the sky.

My favorite Singer

musica

Music

danza

Dance

mangiare

Eat

ascolta

Listen

musica

muzyka

danza

taniec

mangiare

jeść

ascolta

słuchać

Reading Comprehension

My favorite Singer

My name is Jame. I am 10 years old. Michael Jackson is my favorite singer. I love all of his music. He has a great voice. I love to dance to Michael Jackson's music. Every morning, I listen to his music. I listen to his music while eating breakfast. Michael Jackson is the best!

The text is about

A. eating breakfast with Michael Jackson

B. dancing to Michael Jackson's music

C. Jame's favorite singer, Michael Jackson

A detail that tells about the main idea is

A. Michael Jackson is 11 years old.

B. Jame dances to Michael Jackson's music.

C. James eats breakfast alone.

Excellent Trip to the Zoo

animali

Animals

zoo

Zoo

banana

Banana

giraffa

Giraffe

Excellent Trip to the Zoo

animali

Zwierząt

zoo

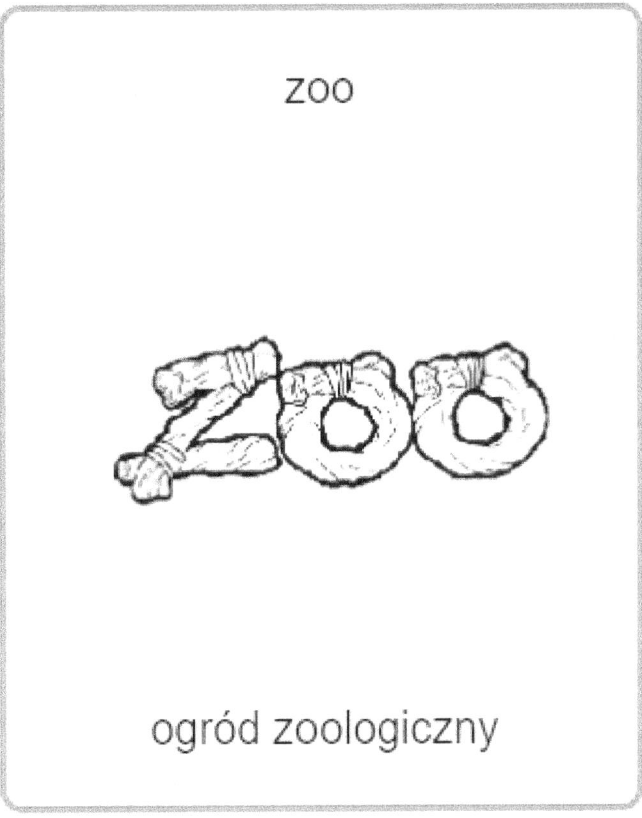

ogród zoologiczny

banana

banan

giraffa

żyrafa

Excellent Trip to the Zoo

Tim visited the zoo with his brother Tom. He saw many animals there. Most of the animals were in open enclosures. Tim was allowed to feed the animals. He chose to feed the monkeys. He gave the monkeys some bananas. It was a lot of fun.

The text is about

A. feeding monkeys

B. animals at the zoo

C. Tim and Tom's visit to the zoo.

A detail that tells about the main idea is

A. Tom fed a giraffe.

B. Tim fed the monkeys bananas.

C. Tim only saw a few animals.

Great Shopping with My Mommy

mamma

Mom

fiore

Flower

vaso

Vase

nonna

Grandmother

Great Shopping with My Mommy

mamma

mama

fiore

kwiat

vaso

wazon

nonna

babcia

Great Shopping with My Mommy

Abby loves shopping with her mommy. Today she went to buy flowers with her mommy. At the florist, Abby saw many different flowers. The flowers were of various colors. Abby helped her mommy choose some pink and red flowers for their vase. Her mother also bought some yellow and blue flowers for Abby's grandmother.

The text is about

A. pink and red flowers

B. shopping with mommy

C. shopping for flowers with mommy

A detail that tells about the main idea is

A. Abby did not want to go shopping.

B. Abby saw only yellow and blue flowers.

C. Abby chose pink and red flowers for her mommy.

My Gorgeous Garden

pianta

Plant

rosa

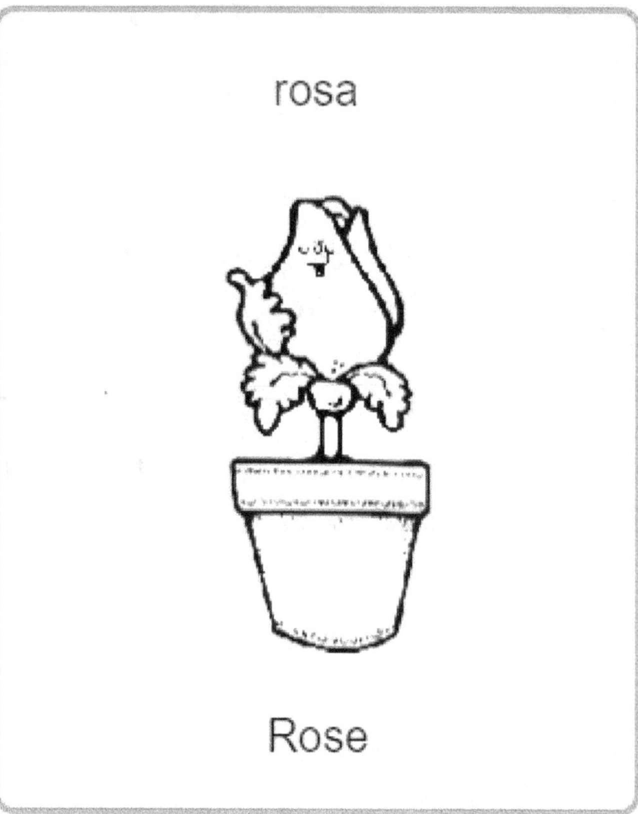

Rose

girasole

Sunflower

giardino

Garden

My Gorgeous Garden

pianta

roślina

rosa

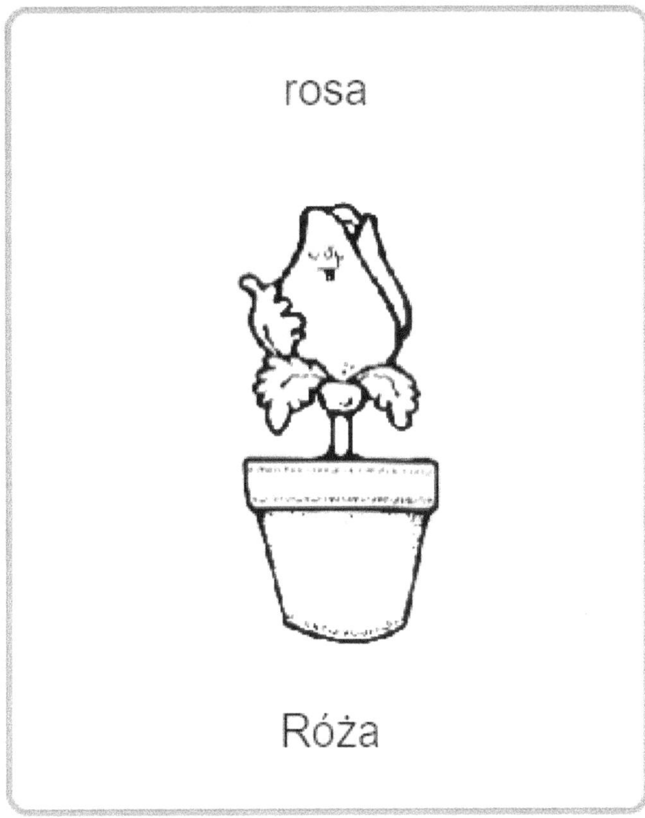

Róża

girasole

słonecznik

giardino

ogród

My Gorgeous Garden

My name is Pimmy. I have a gorgeous garden at my house. I water the plants in my garden every morning. I have a rose plant in my garden. It is a white rose plant. I also have sunflowers in the garden. I am going to plant more things in my garden.

The text is about

A. Pimmy's beautiful garden

B. A rose garden

C. sunflowers in the garden

A detail that tells about the main idea is

A. Pimmy has white roses in her garden.

B. Pimmy has red roses in her garden.

C. Pimmy waters her garden once a week.

Q1: A Q2: A

Black Beauty Horse

cavallo

Horse

cavalcate

Ride

veloce

Fast

lento

Slow

Black Beauty Horse

cavallo

koń

cavalcate

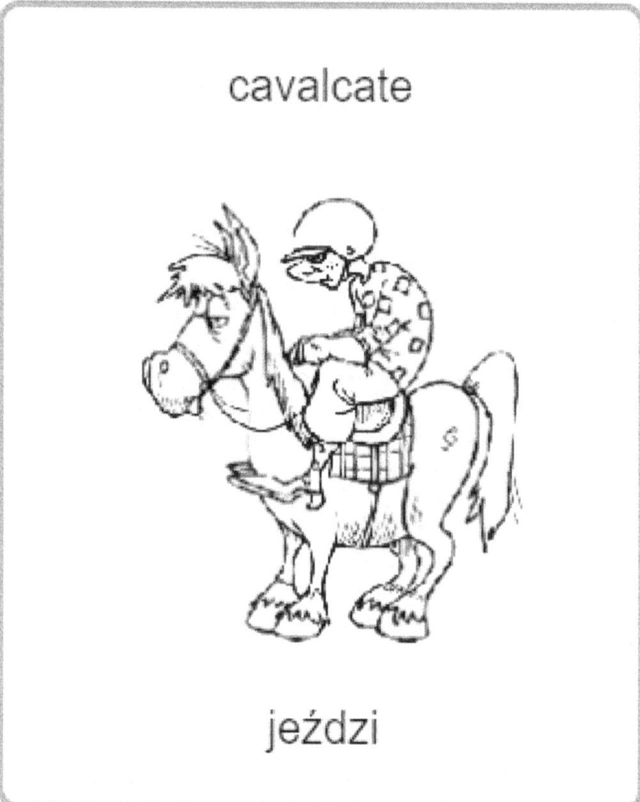

jeździ

veloce

szybki

lento

powolny

Reading Comprehension

Black Beauty Horse

Laura loves horses. She names her horse Black Beauty. It is a black and elegant horse. It is also a friendly and loving horse. It can go very fast. When Laura rides Black Beauty, she feels happy. Laura rides her horse once every week.

The text is about

A. black horses

B. fast horses

C. Luara's horse Black Beauty

A detail that tells about the main idea is

A. Black Beauty is a friendly horse.

B. Black Beauty is a slow-moving horse.

C. Laura is afraid to ride her horse.

The First Day to School

borsa

Bag

libro

Book

scarpe

Shoes

calzini

Socks

The First Day to School

borsa

torba

libro

książka

scarpe

buty

calzini

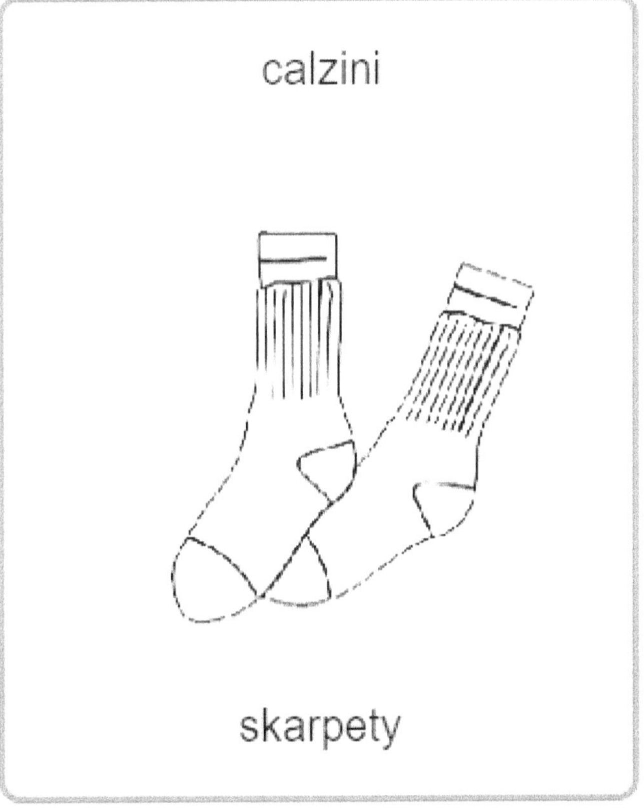

skarpety

The First Day to School

Today is Esther's first day of school. She is very nervous. Her mother bought her a new school backpack. It is a big pink and blue backpack. She has new books in her backpack. Esther also has a new school uniform. Her shoes and socks are bright white. Esther is ready for her first day of school.

The text is about

A. a new school backpack

B. Esther's first day at school

C. getting ready for school every morning

A detail that tells about the main idea is

A. Esther has a new pink and blue school backpack.

B. Esther's shoes are black.

C. Esther likes to go to school.

Be Ready for the Adventure Camp

boy scout

Boy Scout

campeggio

Camping

tenda

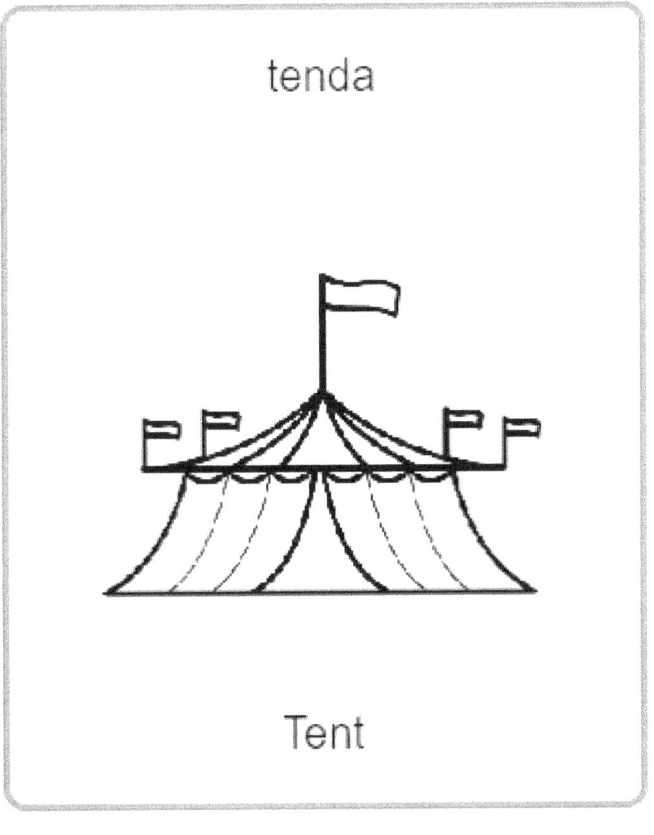

Tent

giungla

Jungle

boy scout

skaut

campeggio

kemping

tenda

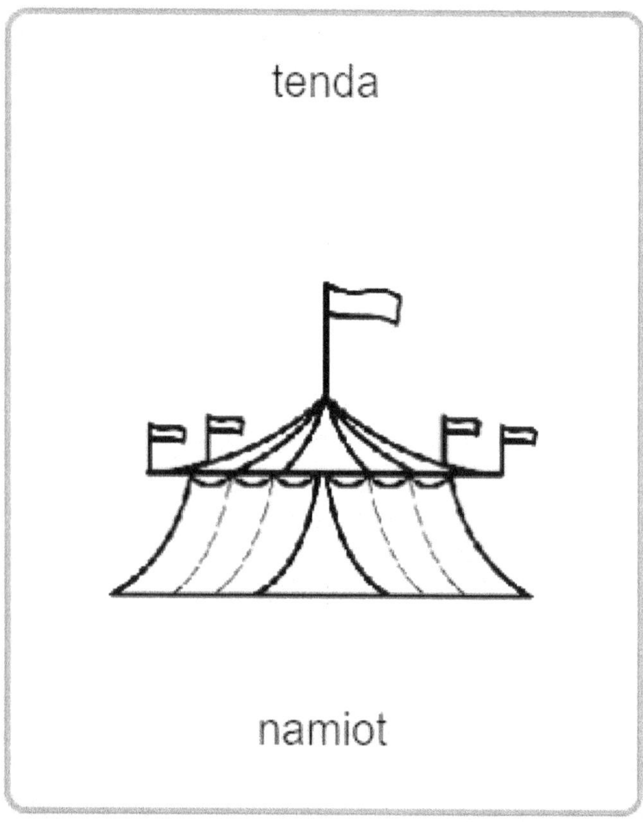

namiot

giungla

dżungla

Be Ready for the Adventure Camp

The scouts are going camping this weekend. They have to make sure they bring all the essential things. They have to bring their own camping tents. All the s outs are excited about their camping trip. They are looking forward to the weekend.

The text is about

A. scouts camping in the jungle

B. scouts getting ready for a camping trip

C. scouts having fun

A detail that tells about the main idea is

A. The scouts are worried about the trip.

B. The scouts need to buy sleeping bags.

C. The scouts need to bring their own camping tents.

Marvelous Time at the Funfair

fratello

Brother

ridere

Laugh

caramella

Candy

sedersi

Sit

Marvelous Time at the Funfair

fratello

brat

ridere

śmiech

caramella

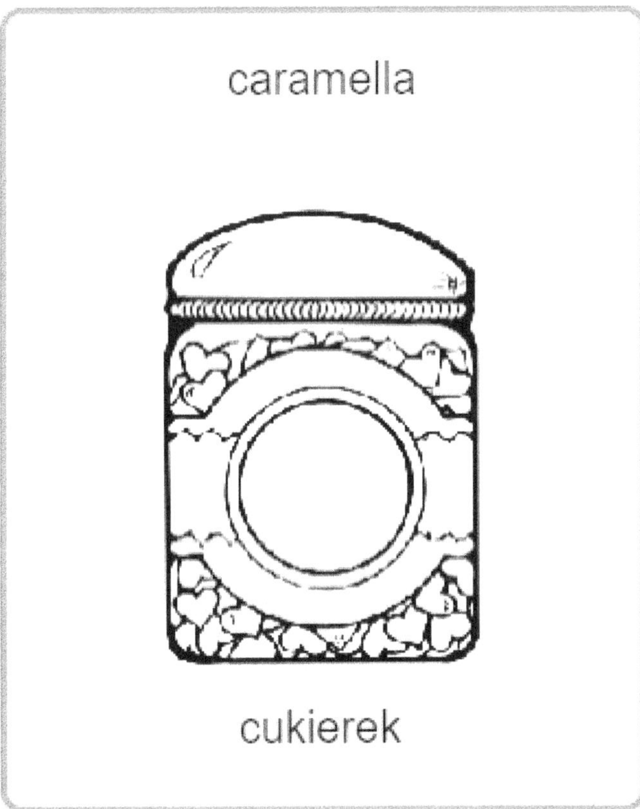

cukierek

sedersi

siedzieć

Reading Comprehension

Marvelous Time at the Funfair

The funfair is near Nathan's home. Every day Nathan visits the funfair with his older brother, Nay. He loves to sit on the Ferris wheel with Nay. You can hear them laughing as they go up the Ferris wheel. At the funfair, Nay buys Nathan his favorite yummy candy. He becomes thrilled after visiting the funfair.

The text is about

A. funfair

B. riding the Ferris wheel

C. Nathan enjoying the funfair

A detail that tells about the main idea is

A. Nathan is tired after visiting the funfair.

B. Nathan and Nay laugh on the Ferris wheel.

C. Nathan takes good care of Nay at the funfair.

Prepare for a Feast

mercato

Market

pesce

Fish

granchio

Crab

cucinare

Cook

Prepare for a Feast

mercato

rynek

pesce

ryba

granchio

Krab

cucinare

gotować

Prepare for a Feast

Today is Sunday. In the morning, I go to the fresh market with my mom. She buys many things in the market. First, my mom buys two big fishes. Next, she gets a big bag of prawns and a small bag of crabs. I cannot wait for my mom to get home to start cooking. Lunch is going to be a feast.

The text is about

A. cooking crabs

B. lunch being a feast

C. going to the market with mom

A detail that tells about the main idea is

A. Mom buys two big fishes.

B. Mom cooks crabs for dinner.

C. Mom buys two big bags of prawns.

Pleasure Time on Airplane

aereo

Airplane

televisione

Television

succo

Juice

cartone animato

Cartoon

Pleasure Time on Airplane

aereo

samolot

televisione

telewizja

succo

sok

cartone animato

kreskówka

Reading Comprehension

Pleasure Time on Airplane

This is my first time on an airplane. It is very big. It has many seats. There are small television screens behind each seat. I can watch cartoons on the screen. They serve me food and drinks. I have orange juice with my sandwich. I like traveling on an airplane.

The text is about

A. eating on an airplane

B. my first trip on an airplane

C. watching cartoons on an airplane

A detail that tells about the main idea is

A. An airplane has few seats.

B. There is no food on an airplane.

C. I can watch cartoons on an airplane.

Toys Everywhere

treni

Trains

auto

Car

padre

Father

ape

Bee

Toys Everywhere

treni

pociągi

auto

samochód

padre

ojciec

ape

pszczoła

Reading Comprehension

Toys Everywhere

I visited the toy shop today. There were numerous toys on sale. There were trains, buses, airplanes, and cars. My father said I could pick only one toy. I really wanted a toy car. I chose a great yellow toy car. It reminded me of a bumblebee. I named my car Bumble Bee

The text is about

A. a toy car

B. a bumblebee

C. a toy shop

A detail that tells about the main idea is

A. The toy shop only had cars.

B. The toy shop had a yellow toy car.

C. The toy shop had to bumblebees.

The Dream Animals Farm

pollo

Chicken

capra

Goat

mucca

Cow

anatra

Duck

The Dream Animals Farm

pollo

kurczak

capra

Koza

mucca

krowa

anatra

kaczka

The Dream Animals Farm

Jenny visited an animal farm yesterday. On the farm, she saw several animals. There were chickens, goats, cows, ducks, and horses on the farm. The farmer let Jenny play with all the animals. Jenny helped him feed the animals. She was delighted she could help with the animals. Jenny wishes she can visit again sometime.

The text is about

A. farm animals

B. feeding animals

C. Jenny's farm visit.

A detail that tells about the main idea is

A. Jenny rode animals on the farm.

B. Jenny helped to feed the animals.

C. Jenny does not want to go back to the farm.

www.ingramcontent.com/pod-product-compliance
Lightning Source LLC
Chambersburg PA
CBHW081929120726
47997CB00010B/3092